DR. JEKYLL
AND MR. HYDE

Robert Louis Stevenson

TECHNICAL DIRECTOR Maxwell Krohn
EDITORIAL DIRECTOR Justin Kestler
MANAGING EDITOR Ben Florman

SERIES EDITORS Boomie Aglietti, Justin Kestler
PRODUCTION Christian Lorentzen

WRITERS Ross Douthat, Benjamin Lytal
EDITORS Katie Mannheimer, Dennis Quinio

This edition published by Spark Publishing

Spark Publishing
A Division of SparkNotes LLC
120 Fifth Avenue, 8th Floor
New York, NY 10011

02 03 04 05 SN 9 8 7 6 5 4 3 2 1

Please send all comments and questions or report errors to
feedback@sparknotes.com.

Library of Congress information available upon request

Printed and bound in the United States

RRD-C

ISBN 1-58663-509-3

INTRODUCTION: STOPPING TO BUY SPARKNOTES ON A SNOWY EVENING

Whose words these are you *think* you know.
Your paper's due tomorrow, though;
We're glad to see you stopping here
To get some help before you go.

Lost your course? You'll find it here.
Face tests and essays without fear.
Between the words, good grades at stake:
Get great results throughout the year.

Once school bells caused your heart to quake
As teachers circled each mistake.
Use SparkNotes and no longer weep,
Ace every single test you take.

Yes, books are lovely, dark, and deep,
But only what you grasp you keep,
With hours to go before you sleep,
With hours to go before you sleep.

Contents

NOTE: This SparkNote uses the Signet Classic edition of *Dr. Jekyll and Mr. Hyde*. Stevenson's novel does not use chapter numbers; the separate sections simply appear with brief descriptive headings, starting with "Story of the Door." For convenience of reference, this SparkNote has assigned a number to each chapter; the numbers do not reflect Stevenson's own system of organization.

CONTEXT

R OBERT LOUIS STEVENSON, ONE OF THE MASTERS OF
the Victorian adventure story, was born in Edin-
burgh, Scotland, on November 13, 1850. He was a
sickly child, and respiratory troubles plagued him
throughout his life. As a young man, he traveled
through Europe, leading a bohemian lifestyle and penning his first
two books, both travel narratives. In 1876, he met a married
woman, Fanny Van de Grift Osbourne, and fell in love with her.
Mrs. Osbourne eventually divorced her husband, and she and
Stevenson were married.

Stevenson returned to London with his bride and wrote prolifi-
cally over the next decade, in spite of his terrible health. He won
widespread admiration with *Treasure Island,* written in 1883, and
followed it with *Kidnapped* in 1886; both were adventure stories,
the former a pirate tale set on the high seas and the latter a historical
novel set in Stevenson's native Scotland. *Dr. Jekyll and Mr. Hyde,*
which Stevenson described as a "fine bogey tale," also came out in
1886. It met with tremendous success, selling 40,000 copies in six
months and ensuring Stevenson's fame as a writer.

In its narrative of a respectable doctor who transforms himself
into a savage murderer, *Dr. Jekyll and Mr. Hyde* tapped directly into
the anxieties of Stevenson's age. The Victorian era, named for
Queen Victoria, who ruled England for most of the nineteenth century, was a time of unprecedented technological progress and an age
in which European nations carved up the world with their empires.
By the end of the century, however, many people were beginning to
call into question the ideals of progress and civilization that had
defined the era, and a growing sense of pessimism and decline per-
vaded artistic circles. Many felt that the end of the century was also
witnessing a twilight of Western culture.

With the notion of a single body containing both the erudite Dr.
Jekyll and the depraved Mr. Hyde, Stevenson's novel imagines an
inextricable link between civilization and savagery, good and evil.
Jekyll's attraction to the freedom from restraint that Hyde enjoys
mirrors Victorian England's secret attraction to allegedly savage
non-Western cultures, even as Europe claimed superiority over
them. This attraction also informs such books as Joseph Conrad's

Heart of Darkness. For, as the Western world came in contact with other peoples and ways of life, it found aspects of these cultures within itself, and both desired and feared to indulge them. These aspects included open sensuality, physicality, and other so-called irrational tendencies. Even as Victorian England sought to assert its civilization over and against these instinctual sides of life, it found them secretly fascinating. Indeed, society's repression of its darker side only increased the fascination. As a product of this society, *Dr. Jekyll and Mr. Hyde* manifests this fascination; yet, as a work of art, it also questions this interest.

By the late 1880s, Stevenson had become one of the leading lights of English literature. But even after garnering fame, he led a somewhat troubled life. He traveled often, seeking to find a climate more amenable to the tuberculosis that haunted his later days. Eventually he settled in Samoa, and there Stevenson died suddenly in 1894, at the age of forty-four.

PLOT OVERVIEW

O**N THEIR WEEKLY WALK,** an eminently sensible, trustworthy lawyer named Mr. Utterson listens as his friend Enfield tells a gruesome tale of assault. The tale describes a sinister figure named Mr. Hyde who tramples a young girl, disappears into a door on the street, and reemerges to pay off her relatives with a check signed by a respectable gentleman. Since both Utterson and Enfield disapprove of gossip, they agree to speak no further of the matter. It happens, however, that one of Utterson's clients and close friends, Dr. Jekyll, has written a will transferring all of his property to this same Mr. Hyde. Soon, Utterson begins having dreams in which a faceless figure stalks through a nightmarish version of London.

Puzzled, the lawyer visits Jekyll and their mutual friend Dr. Lanyon to try to learn more. Lanyon reports that he no longer sees much of Jekyll, since they had a dispute over the course of Jekyll's research, which Lanyon calls "unscientific balderdash." Curious, Utterson stakes out a building that Hyde visits—which, it turns out, is a laboratory attached to the back of Jekyll's home. Encountering Hyde, Utterson is amazed by how undefinably ugly the man seems, as if deformed, though Utterson cannot say exactly how. Much to Utterson's surprise, Hyde willingly offers Utterson his address. Jekyll tells Utterson not to concern himself with the matter of Hyde.

A year passes uneventfully. Then, one night, a servant girl witnesses Hyde brutally beat to death an old man named Sir Danvers Carew, a member of Parliament and a client of Utterson. The police contact Utterson, and Utterson suspects Hyde as the murderer. He leads the officers to Hyde's apartment, feeling a sense of foreboding amid the eerie weather—the morning is dark and wreathed in fog. When they arrive at the apartment, the murderer has vanished, and police searches prove futile. Shortly thereafter, Utterson again visits Jekyll, who now claims to have ended all relations with Hyde; he shows Utterson a note, allegedly written to Jekyll by Hyde, apologizing for the trouble he has caused him and saying goodbye. That night, however, Utterson's clerk points out that Hyde's handwriting bears a remarkable similarity to Jekyll's own.

For a few months, Jekyll acts especially friendly and sociable, as if a weight has been lifted from his shoulders. But then Jekyll suddenly begins to refuse visitors, and Lanyon dies from some kind of shock he received in connection with Jekyll. Before dying, however, Lanyon gives Utterson a letter, with instructions that he not open it until after Jekyll's death. Meanwhile, Utterson goes out walking with Enfield, and they see Jekyll at a window of his laboratory; the three men begin to converse, but a look of horror comes over Jekyll's face, and he slams the window and disappears. Soon afterward, Jekyll's butler, Mr. Poole, visits Utterson in a state of desperation: Jekyll has secluded himself in his laboratory for several weeks, and now the voice that comes from the room sounds nothing like the doctor's. Utterson and Poole travel to Jekyll's house through empty, windswept, sinister streets; once there, they find the servants huddled together in fear. After arguing for a time, the two of them resolve to break into Jekyll's laboratory. Inside, they find the body of Hyde, wearing Jekyll's clothes and apparently dead by suicide—and a letter from Jekyll to Utterson promising to explain everything.

Utterson takes the document home, where first he reads Lanyon's letter; it reveals that Lanyon's deterioration and eventual death were caused by the shock of seeing Mr. Hyde take a potion and metamorphose into Dr. Jekyll. The second letter constitutes a testament by Jekyll. It explains how Jekyll, seeking to separate his good side from his darker impulses, discovered a way to transform himself periodically into a deformed monster free of conscience—Mr. Hyde. At first, Jekyll reports, he delighted in becoming Hyde and rejoiced in the moral freedom that the creature possessed. Eventually, however, he found that he was turning into Hyde involuntarily in his sleep, even without taking the potion. At this point, Jekyll resolved to cease becoming Hyde. One night, however, the urge gripped him too strongly, and after the transformation he immediately rushed out and violently killed Sir Danvers Carew. Horrified, Jekyll tried more adamantly to stop the transformations, and for a time he proved successful; one day, however, while sitting in a park, he suddenly turned into Hyde, the first time that an involuntary metamorphosis had happened while he was awake.

The letter continues describing Jekyll's cry for help. Far from his laboratory and hunted by the police as a murderer, Hyde needed Lanyon's help to get his potions and become Jekyll again—but when he undertook the transformation in Lanyon's presence, the shock of the sight instigated Lanyon's deterioration and death. Meanwhile, Jekyll returned to his home, only to find himself ever more helpless and trapped as the transformations increased in frequency and

necessitated even larger doses of potion in order to reverse themselves. It was the onset of one of these spontaneous metamorphoses
that caused Jekyll to slam his laboratory window shut in the middle
of his conversation with Enfield and Utterson. Eventually, the
potion began to run out, and Jekyll was unable to find a key ingredient to make more. His ability to change back from Hyde into
Jekyll slowly vanished. Jekyll writes that even as he composes his
letter he knows that he will soon become Hyde permanently, and he
wonders if Hyde will face execution for his crimes or choose to kill
himself. Jekyll notes that, in any case, the end of his letter marks the
end of the life of Dr. Jekyll. With these words, both the document
and the novel come to a close.

Character List

Dr. Henry Jekyll A respected doctor and friend of both Lanyon, a
    fellow physician, and Utterson, a lawyer. Jekyll is a
    seemingly prosperous man, well established in the
    community, and known for his decency and charitable
    works. Since his youth, however, he has secretly
    engaged in unspecified dissolute and corrupt behavior.
    Jekyll finds this dark side a burden and undertakes
    experiments intended to separate his good and evil
    selves from one another. Through these experiments,
    he brings Mr. Hyde into being, finding a way to
    transform himself in such a way that he fully becomes
    his darker half.

Mr. Edward Hyde A strange, repugnant man who looks faintly
    pre-human. Hyde is violent and cruel, and everyone
    who sees him describes him as ugly and deformed—yet
    no one can say exactly why. Language itself seems to
    fail around Hyde: he is not a creature who belongs to
    the rational world, the world of conscious articulation
    or logical grammar. Hyde is Jekyll's dark side, released
    from the bonds of conscience and loosed into the world
    by a mysterious potion.

Mr. Gabriel John Utterson A prominent and upstanding
    lawyer, well respected in the London community.
    Utterson is reserved, dignified, and perhaps even
    lacking somewhat in imagination, but he does seem
    to possess a furtive curiosity about the more sordid
    side of life. His rationalism, however, makes him ill
    equipped to deal with the supernatural nature of the
    Jekyll-Hyde connection. While not a man of science,
    Utterson resembles his friend Dr. Lanyon—and
    perhaps Victorian society at large—in his devotion
    to reasonable explanations and his denial of
    the supernatural.

Dr. Hastie Lanyon A reputable London doctor and, along with Utterson, formerly one of Jekyll's closest friends. As an embodiment of rationalism, materialism, and skepticism, Lanyon serves a foil (a character whose attitudes or emotions contrast with, and thereby illuminate, those of another character) for Jekyll, who embraces mysticism. His death represents the more general victory of supernaturalism over materialism in *Dr. Jekyll and Mr. Hyde.*

Mr. Poole Jekyll's butler. Mr. Poole is a loyal servant, having worked for the doctor for twenty years, and his concern for his master eventually drives him to seek Utterson's help when he becomes convinced that something has happened to Jekyll.

Mr. Enfield A distant cousin and lifelong friend of Mr. Utterson. Like Utterson, Enfield is reserved, formal, and scornful of gossip; indeed, the two men often walk together for long stretches without saying a word to one another.

Mr. Guest Utterson's clerk and confidant. Guest is also an expert in handwriting. His skill proves particularly useful when Utterson wants him to examine a bit of Hyde's handwriting. Guest notices that Hyde's script is the same as Jekyll's, but slanted the other way.

Sir Danvers Carew A well-liked old nobleman, a member of Parliament, and a client of Utterson.

ANALYSIS OF MAJOR CHARACTERS

DR. JEKYLL & MR. HYDE

One might question the extent to which Dr. Jekyll and Mr. Hyde are in fact a single character. Until the end of the novel, the two personas seem nothing alike—the well-liked, respectable doctor and the hideous, depraved Hyde are almost opposite in type and personality. Stevenson uses this marked contrast to make his point: every human being contains opposite forces within him or her, an alter ego that hides behind one's polite facade. Correspondingly, to understand fully the significance of either Jekyll or Hyde, we must ultimately consider the two as constituting one single character. Indeed, taken alone, neither is a very interesting personality; it is the nature of their interrelationship that gives the novel its power.

Despite the seeming diametric opposition between Dr. Jekyll and Mr. Hyde, their relationship in fact involves a complicated dynamic. While it is true that Jekyll largely appears as moral and decent, engaging in charity work and enjoying a reputation as a courteous and genial man, he in fact never fully embodies virtue in the way that Hyde embodies evil. Although Jekyll undertakes his experiments with the intent of purifying his good side from his bad and vice versa, he ends up separating the bad alone, while leaving his former self, his Jekyll-self, as mixed as before. Jekyll succeeds in liberating his darker side, freeing it from the bonds of conscience, yet as Jekyll he never liberates himself from this darkness.

Jekyll's partial success in his endeavors warrants much analysis. Jekyll himself ascribes his lopsided results to his state of mind when first taking the potion. He says that he was motivated by dark urges such as ambition and pride when he first drank the liquid and that these allowed for the emergence of Hyde. He seems to imply that, had he entered the experiment with pure motives, an angelic being would have emerged. However, one must consider the subsequent events in the novel before acquitting Jekyll of any blame. For, once released, Hyde gradually comes to dominate both personas, until Jekyll takes Hyde's shape more often than his own. Indeed, by the very end of the novel, Jekyll himself no longer exists and only Hyde remains. Hyde seems to possess a force more powerful than Jekyll originally believed. The fact that Hyde, rather than some beatific creature, emerged from Jekyll's experiments seems more than a chance event, subject to an arbitrary state of mind. Rather, Jekyll's drinking of the potion seems almost to have afforded Hyde the opportunity to assert himself. It is as if Hyde, but no comparable virtuous essence, was lying in wait.

This dominance of Hyde—first as a latent force within Jekyll, then as a tyrannical external force subverting Jekyll—holds various implications for our understanding of human nature. We begin to wonder whether any aspect of human nature in fact stands as a counter to an individual's Hyde-like side. We may recall that Hyde is described as resembling a "troglodyte," or a primitive creature; perhaps Hyde is actually the original, authentic nature of man, which has been repressed but not destroyed by the accumulated weight of civilization, conscience, and societal norms. Perhaps man doesn't have two natures but rather a single, primitive, amoral one that remains just barely constrained by the bonds of civilization. Moreover, the novel suggests that once those bonds are broken, it becomes impossible to reestablish them; the genie cannot be put back into the bottle, and eventually Hyde will permanently replace Jekyll—as he finally does. Even in Victorian England—which considered itself the height of Western civilization—Stevenson suggests that the dark, instinctual side of man remains strong enough to devour anyone who, like Jekyll, proves foolish enough to unleash it.

MR. GABRIEL JOHN UTTERSON

Although Utterson witnesses a string of shocking events, Utterson himself is a largely unexciting character and is clearly not a man of strong passions or sensibilities. Indeed, Stevenson intends for him to come across in this way: from the first page of the novel, the text notes that Utterson has a face that is "never lighted by a smile," that he speaks very little, and that he seems "lean, long, dusty, [and] dreary." Yet, somehow, he is also "lovable," and dull and proper though he may be, he has many friends. His lovability may stem from the only interesting quality that Stevenson gives him—namely, his willingness to remain friends with someone whose reputation has suffered. This loyalty leads him to plumb the mystery that surrounds Jekyll.

Utterson represents the perfect Victorian gentleman. He consistently seeks to preserve order and decorum, does not gossip, and guards his friends' reputations as though they were his own. Even when he suspects his friend Jekyll of criminal activities such as blackmail or the sheltering of a murderer, he prefers to sweep what he has learned—or what he thinks he has learned—under the rug rather than bring ruin upon his good friend.

Utterson's status as the epitome of Victorian norms also stems from his devotion to reason and common sense. He investigates what becomes a supernatural sequence of events but never allows himself to even entertain the notion that something uncanny may be going on. He considers that misdeeds may be occurring but not that the mystical or metaphysical might be afoot. Thus, even at the end, when he is summoned by Poole to Jekyll's home and all the servants are gathered frightened in the hallway, Utterson continues to look for an explanation that preserves reason. He desperately searches for excuses not to take any drastic steps to interfere with Jekyll's life. In Utterson's devotion to both decorum and reason, Stevenson depicts Victorian society's general attempt to maintain the authority of civilization over and against humanity's darker side. Stevenson suggests that just as Utterson prefers the suppression or avoidance of revelations to the scandal or chaos that the truth might unleash, so too does Victorian society prefer to repress and deny the existence of an uncivilized or savage element of humanity, no matter how intrinsic that element may be.

Yet, even as Utterson adheres rigidly to order and rationality, he does not fail to notice the uncanny quality of the events he investigates. Indeed, because we see the novel through Utterson's eyes, Stevenson cannot allow Utterson to be *too* unimaginative—otherwise the novel's eerie mood would suffer. Correspondingly, Stevenson attributes nightmares to Utterson and grants him ominous premonitions as he moves through the city at night—neither of which seem to suit the lawyer's normally reasonable personality, which is rarely given to flights of fancy. Perhaps, the novel suggests, the chilling presence of Hyde in London is strong enough to penetrate even the rigidly rational shell that surrounds Utterson, planting a seed of supernatural dread.

DR. HASTIE LANYON

Lanyon plays only a minor role in the novel's plot, but his thematic significance extends beyond his brief appearances. When we first encounter him, he speaks dismissively of Jekyll's experiments, referring to them as "unscientific balderdash." His scientific skepticism renders him, to an even greater extent than Utterson, an embodiment of rationalism and a proponent of materialist explanations. As such, he functions as a kind of foil for Jekyll. Both men are doctors, well respected and successful, but they have chosen divergent paths. From Lanyon's early remarks, we learn that Jekyll shared some of his research with Lanyon, and one may even imagine that they were partners at one point. But Lanyon chooses to engage in rational, materialist science, while Jekyll prefers to pursue what might be called mystical or metaphysical science.

It is appropriate, then, that Lanyon is the first person to see Jekyll enact his transformations—the great advocate of material causes is witness to undeniable proof of a metaphysical, physically impossible phenomenon. Having spent his life as a rationalist and a skeptic, Lanyon cannot deal with the world that Jekyll's experiments have revealed. Deep within himself, Lanyon prefers to die rather than go on living in a universe that, from his point of view, has been turned upside down. After his cataclysmic experience, Lanyon, who has spent his life pursuing knowledge, explicitly rejects the latest knowledge he has gained. "I sometimes think if we knew all," he tells Utterson, "we should be more glad to get away." With these words, Lanyon departs from the novel, his uncompromising rationalism ceding to the inexplicable reality of Jekyll.

THEMES, MOTIFS & SYMBOLS

THEMES

Themes are the fundamental and often universal ideas explored in a literary work.

THE DUALITY OF HUMAN NATURE

Dr. Jekyll and Mr. Hyde centers upon a conception of humanity as dual in nature, although the theme does not emerge fully until the last chapter, when the complete story of the Jekyll-Hyde relationship is revealed. Therefore, we confront the theory of a dual human nature explicitly only after having witnessed all of the events of the novel, including Hyde's crimes and his ultimate eclipsing of Jekyll. The text not only posits the duality of human nature as its central theme but forces us to ponder the properties of this duality and to consider each of the novel's episodes as we weigh various theories.

Jekyll asserts that "man is not truly one, but truly two," and he imagines the human soul as the battleground for an "angel" and a "fiend," each struggling for mastery. But his potion, which he hoped would separate and purify each element, succeeds only in bringing the dark side into being—Hyde emerges, but he has no angelic counterpart. Once unleashed, Hyde slowly takes over, until Jekyll ceases to exist. If man is half angel and half fiend, one wonders what happens to the "angel" at the end of the novel.

Perhaps the angel gives way permanently to Jekyll's devil. Or perhaps Jekyll is simply mistaken: man is not "truly two" but is first and foremost the primitive creature embodied in Hyde, brought under tentative control by civilization, law, and conscience. According to this theory, the potion simply strips away the civilized veneer, exposing man's essential nature. Certainly, the novel goes out of its way to paint Hyde as animalistic—he is hairy and ugly; he conducts himself according to instinct rather than reason; Utterson describes him as a "troglodyte," or primitive creature.

Yet if Hyde were just an animal, we would not expect him to take such *delight* in crime. Indeed, he seems to commit violent acts against innocents for no reason except the joy of it—something that no animal would do. He appears deliberately and happily *im*moral rather than *a*moral; he knows the moral law and basks in his breach of it. For an animalistic creature, furthermore, Hyde seems oddly at home in the urban landscape. All of these observations imply that perhaps civilization, too, has its dark side.

Ultimately, while Stevenson clearly asserts human nature as possessing two aspects, he leaves open the question of what these aspects constitute. Perhaps they consist of evil and virtue; perhaps they represent one's inner animal and the veneer that civilization has imposed. Stevenson enhances the richness of the novel by leaving us to look within ourselves to find the answers.

THE IMPORTANCE OF REPUTATION

For the characters in *Dr. Jekyll and Mr. Hyde,* preserving one's reputation emerges as all important. The prevalence of this value system is evident in the way that upright men such as Utterson and Enfield avoid gossip at all costs; they see gossip as a great destroyer of reputation. Similarly, when Utterson suspects Jekyll first of being blackmailed and then of sheltering Hyde from the police, he does not make his suspicions known; part of being Jekyll's good friend is a willingness to keep his secrets and not ruin his respectability. The importance of reputation in the novel also reflects the importance of appearances, facades, and surfaces, which often hide a sordid underside. In many instances in the novel, Utterson, true to his Victorian society, adamantly wishes not only to preserve Jekyll's reputation but also to preserve the appearance of order and decorum, even as he senses a vile truth lurking underneath.

MOTIFS

> *Motifs are recurring structures, contrasts, or literary devices that can help to develop and inform the text's major themes.*

VIOLENCE AGAINST INNOCENTS

The text repeatedly depicts Hyde as a creature of great evil and countless vices. Although the reader learns the details of only two of Hyde's crimes, the nature of both underlines his depravity. Both involve violence directed against innocents in particular. In the first instance, the victim of Hyde's violence is a small, female child; in the second instance, it is a gentle and much-beloved old man. The fact that Hyde ruthlessly murders these harmless beings, who have seemingly done nothing to provoke his rage and even less to deserve death, emphasizes the extreme immorality of Jekyll's dark side unleashed. Hyde's brand of evil constitutes not just a lapse from good but an outright attack on it.

SILENCE

Repeatedly in the novel, characters fail or refuse to articulate themselves. Either they seem unable to describe a horrifying perception, such as the physical characteristics of Hyde, or they deliberately abort or avoid certain conversations. Enfield and Utterson cut off their discussion of Hyde in the first chapter out of a distaste for gossip; Utterson refuses to share his suspicions about Jekyll throughout his investigation of his client's predicament. Moreover, neither Jekyll in his final confession nor the third-person narrator in the rest of the novel ever provides any details of Hyde's sordid behavior and secret vices. It is unclear whether these narrative silences owe to a failure of language or a refusal to use it.

Ultimately, the two kinds of silence in the novel indicate two different notions about the interaction of the rational and the irrational. The characters' refusals to discuss the sordid indicate an attribute of the Victorian society in which they live. This society prizes decorum and reputation above all and prefers to repress or even deny the truth if that truth threatens to upset the conventionally ordered worldview. Faced with the irrational, Victorian society and its inhabitants prefer not to acknowledge its presence and not to grant it the legitimacy of a name. Involuntary silences, on the other hand, imply something about language itself. Language is by nature rational and logical, a method by which we map and delineate our world. Perhaps when confronted with the irrational and the mystical, language itself simply breaks down. Perhaps something about verbal expression stands at odds with the supernatural. Interestingly, certain parts of the novel suggest that, in the clash between language and the uncanny, the uncanny need not always win. One can interpret Stevenson's reticence on the topic of Jekyll's and Hyde's crimes as a conscious choice not to defuse their chilling aura with descriptions that might only dull them.

URBAN TERROR

Throughout the novel, Stevenson goes out of his way to establish a link between the urban landscape of Victorian London and the dark events surrounding Hyde. He achieves his desired effect through the use of nightmarish imagery, in which dark streets twist and coil, or lie draped in fog, forming a sinister landscape befitting the crimes that take place there. Chilling visions of the city appear in Utterson's nightmares as well, and the text notes that

> He would be aware of the great field of lamps of a nocturnal city. . . . The figure [of Hyde] . . . haunted the lawyer all night; and if at any time he dozed over, it was but to see it glide more stealthily through sleeping houses, or move the more swiftly . . . through wider labyrinths of lamp-lighted city, and at every street corner crush a child and leave her screaming.

In such images, Stevenson paints Hyde as an urban creature, utterly at home in the darkness of London—where countless crimes take place, the novel suggests, without anyone knowing.

SYMBOLS

Symbols are objects, characters, figures, or colors used to represent abstract ideas or concepts.

JEKYLL'S HOUSE AND LABORATORY

Dr. Jekyll lives in a well-appointed home, characterized by Stevenson as having "a great air of wealth and comfort." His laboratory is described as "a certain sinister block of building ... [which] bore in every feature the marks of profound and sordid negligence." With its decaying facade and air of neglect, the laboratory quite neatly symbolizes the corrupt and perverse Hyde. Correspondingly, the respectable, prosperous-looking main house symbolizes the respectable, upright Jekyll. Moreover, the connection between the buildings similarly corresponds to the connection between the personas they represent. The buildings are adjoined but look out on two different streets. Because of the convoluted layout of the streets in the area, the casual observer cannot detect that the structures are two parts of a whole, just as he or she would be unable to detect the relationship between Jekyll and Hyde.

HYDE'S PHYSICAL APPEARANCE

According to the indefinite remarks made by his overwhelmed observers, Hyde appears repulsively ugly and deformed, small, shrunken, and hairy. His physical ugliness and deformity symbolizes his moral hideousness and warped ethics. Indeed, for the audience of Stevenson's time, the connection between such ugliness and Hyde's wickedness might have been seen as more than symbolic. Many people believed in the science of physiognomy, which held that one could identify a criminal by physical appearance. Additionally, Hyde's small stature may represent the fact that, as Jekyll's dark side, he has been repressed for years, prevented from growing and flourishing. His hairiness may indicate that he is not so much an evil side of Jekyll as the embodiment of Jekyll's instincts, the animalistic core beneath Jekyll's polished exterior.

SYMBOLS

Summary & Analysis

Chapter 1: "Story of the Door"

SUMMARY

> *Mr. Utterson the lawyer was a man of a rugged*
> *countenance . . . the last good influence in the lives of*
> *down-going men.*   (See QUOTATIONS, p. 43)

Mr. Utterson is a wealthy, well-respected London lawyer, a reserved and perhaps even boring man who nevertheless inspires a strange fondness in those who know him. Despite his eminent respectability, he never abandons a friend whose reputation has been sullied or ruined.

Utterson nurtures a close friendship with Mr. Enfield, his distant relative and likewise a respectable London gentleman. The two seem to have little in common, and when they take their weekly walk together they often go for quite a distance without saying anything to one another; nevertheless, they look forward to these strolls as one of the high points of the week.

As the story begins, Utterson and Enfield are taking their regular Sunday stroll and walking down a particularly prosperous-looking street. They come upon a neglected building, which seems out of place in the neighborhood, and Enfield relates a story in connection with it. Enfield was walking in the same neighborhood late one night, when he witnessed a shrunken, misshapen man crash into and trample a young girl. He collared the man before he could get away, and then brought him back to the girl, around whom an angry crowd had gathered. The captured man appeared so overwhelmingly ugly that the crowd immediately despised him. United, the crowd threatened to ruin the ugly man's good name unless he did something to make amends; the man, seeing himself trapped, bought them off with one hundred pounds, which he obtained upon entering the neglected building through its only door. Strangely enough, the check bore the name of a very reputable man; furthermore, and in spite of Enfield's suspicions, it proved to be legitimate and not a forgery. Enfield hypothesizes that the ugly culprit had somehow blackmailed the man whose name appeared on the check. Spurning gossip, however, Enfield refuses to reveal that name.

Utterson then asks several pointed questions confirming the details of the incident. Enfield tries to describe the nature of the mysterious man's ugliness but cannot express it, stating, "I never saw a man I so disliked, and yet I scarce know why." He divulges that the culprit's name was Hyde, and, at this point, Utterson declares that he knows the man, and notes that he can now guess the name on the check. But, as the men have just been discussing the virtue of minding one's own business, they promptly agree never to discuss the matter again.

> He is not easy to describe. . . . And it's not want of
> memory; for I declare I can see him this moment.
> (See QUOTATIONS, p. 44)

ANALYSIS

The story of Jekyll and Hyde is one of the most well known in the English language, and few readers come to this novel without knowing the secret behind the relationship of the title characters. Nevertheless, it is important to remember that Stevenson's novel does not reveal this secret until the very end. Instead, the book presents us with what seems like a detective novel, beginning with a sinister figure of unknown origin, a mysterious act of violence, and hints of blackmail and secret scandal. Although the opening scene also contains vaguely supernatural elements, particularly in the strange dread that Hyde inspires, Stevenson likely intended his readers to enter the novel believing it to be nothing more than a mystery story. The uncanny side of the novel appears gradually, as Utterson's detective work leads him toward the seemingly impossible truth.

Even as it plunges us into the mysterious happenings surrounding Mr. Hyde, the first chapter highlights the proper, respectable, eminently Victorian attitudes of Enfield and Utterson. The text describes these men as reserved—so reserved, in fact, that they can enjoy a lengthy walk during which neither man says a word. Declining to indulge their more impulsive thoughts and feelings, they display a mutual distaste for sensation and gossip. They steer away from discussing the matter of Hyde once they realize it involves someone Utterson knows. The Victorian value system largely privileged reputation over reality, and this prioritization is reflected both in the narrator's remarks about Utterson and Enfield and in the characters' own remarks about gossip and blackmail. In a society so focused on reputation, blackmail proves a particularly potent force, since those possessing and concerned with good reputations will do anything they can to preserve them. Thus, when Hyde tramples the little girl, Enfield and the crowd can blackmail him into paying off her family; Hyde's access to a respectable man's bank account leads Enfield to leap to the conclusion that Hyde is blackmailing his benefactor.

In such a society, it is significant that Utterson, so respectable himself, is known for his willingness to remain friends with people whose reputations have been damaged, or ruined. This aspect of his personality suggests not only a sense of charity, but also hints that Utterson is intrigued, in some way, by the darker side of the world—the side that the truly respectable, like Enfield, carefully avoid. It is this curiosity on Utterson's part that leads him to investigate the peculiar figure of Mr. Hyde rather than avoid looking into matters that could touch on scandal.

However, while Utterson may take an interest in affairs that polite society would like to ignore, he remains a steadfast rationalist and a fundamentally unimaginative man without a superstitious bone in his body. One of the central themes of the novel is the clash between Victorian rationalism and the supernatural, and Utterson emerges as the embodiment of this rationality, always searching out the logical explanation for events and deliberately dismissing supernatural flights of fancy. Enfield approaches the world in much the same way, serving as another representative of the commonsense approach. By allowing these men and their Victorian perspectives to dominate the novel's point of view, Stevenson proves better able to dramatize the opposition between the rationalism that they represent and the fantastical subject matter that comes under scrutiny in this focus. However, while this method contributes much to the story's overall effect, it also presents a challenge for Stevenson. The author must struggle to convey to us a sense of metaphysical dread surrounding Hyde, even as he situates his novel's viewpoint with men who never feel such emotions themselves.

In the opening chapter, Stevenson overcomes this challenge by highlighting his characters' inability to express and come to terms with the events that they have witnessed. "There is something wrong with [Hyde's] appearance," Enfield says. "I never saw a man I so disliked, and yet I scarce know why. He must be deformed somewhere; he gives a strong feeling of deformity, although I couldn't specify the point." In other words, Hyde's ugliness is not physical but metaphysical; it attaches to his soul more than to his body. Enfield and, later, Utterson, whose minds are not suited to the metaphysical, can sense Hyde's uncanniness but cannot describe it. Their limited imaginations fail them as they approach the eerie and inexplicable; as rational clashes with irrational, language breaks down.

CHAPTERS 2–3

SUMMARY — CHAPTER 2: "SEARCH FOR MR. HYDE"

Utterson, prompted by his conversation with Enfield, goes home to study a will that he drew up for his close friend Dr. Jekyll. It states that in the event of the death or disappearance of Jekyll, all of his property should be given over immediately to a Mr. Edward Hyde. This strange will had long troubled Utterson, but now that he has heard something of Hyde's behavior, he becomes more upset and feels convinced that Hyde has some peculiar power over Jekyll. Seeking to unravel the mystery, he pays a visit to Dr. Lanyon, a friend of Jekyll's. But Lanyon has never heard of Hyde and has fallen out of communication with Jekyll as a result of a professional dispute. Lanyon refers to Jekyll's most recent line of research as "unscientific balderdash."

Later that night, Utterson is haunted by nightmares in which a faceless man runs down a small child and in which the same terrifying, faceless figure stands beside Jekyll's bed and commands him to rise. Soon, Utterson begins to spend time around the run-down building where Enfield saw Hyde enter, in the hopes of catching a glimpse of Hyde. Hyde, a small young man, finally appears, and Utterson approaches him. Utterson introduces himself as a friend of Henry Jekyll. Hyde, keeping his head down, returns his greetings. He asks Hyde to show him his face, so that he will know him if he sees him again; Hyde complies, and, like Enfield before him, Utterson feels appalled and horrified yet cannot pinpoint exactly what makes Hyde so ugly. Hyde then offers Utterson his address, which the lawyer interprets as a sign that Hyde eagerly anticipates the death of Jekyll and the execution of his will.

After this encounter, Utterson pays a visit to Jekyll. At this point, we learn what Utterson himself has known all along: namely, that the run-down building that Hyde frequents is actually a laboratory attached to Jekyll's well-kept townhouse, which faces outward on a parallel street. Utterson is admitted into Jekyll's home by Jekyll's butler, Mr. Poole, but Jekyll is not at home. Poole tells Utterson that Hyde has a key to the laboratory and that all the servants have orders to obey Hyde. The lawyer heads home, worrying about his friend. He assumes Hyde is blackmailing Jekyll, perhaps for some wrongdoings that Jekyll committed in his youth.

Summary — Chapter 3: "Dr. Jekyll Was Quite at Ease"

Two weeks later, Jekyll throws a well-attended dinner party. Utterson stays late so that the two men can speak privately. Utterson mentions the will, and Jekyll begins to make a joke about it, but he turns pale when Utterson tells him that he has been "learning something of young Hyde." Jekyll explains that the situation with Hyde is exceptional and cannot be solved by talking. He also insists that "the moment I choose, I can be rid of Mr. Hyde." But Jekyll emphasizes the great interest he currently takes in Hyde and his desire to continue to provide for him. He makes Utterson promise that he will carry out his will and testament.

Analysis — Chapters 2–3

Utterson behaves here like an amateur detective, as he does throughout the rest of the novel. However, unlike most detectives, he faces a gulf between what seems to be the factual evidence of the case and the supernatural reality behind it. This gulf is apparent in Utterson's reading of the will, for instance. On the face of it, Jekyll's stipulation that all his property be handed over to Hyde and his later horror at the thought of Utterson "learning something of young Hyde" seem to point squarely at blackmail of some sort. Of course, Utterson never imagines the situation that lies behind these behaviors. Similarly, the will's reference to "death or *disappearance*" (emphasis added) makes Utterson immediately think of the possibility of murder. The idea that Jekyll could literally transform himself into another and thereby disappear simply does not occur to Utterson, as it would not occur to any rational person. Utterson's failure to detect the truth does not demonstrate any failure in logic.

However, Stevenson does contrive to have his hardheaded lawyer access the dark supernatural undercurrents at work in the case of Jekyll and Hyde—if only in a limited way. Stevenson enlightens

Utterson through the use of the dream sequence. In Utterson's dreams, the faceless figure of Hyde stalks through the city: "if at any time [Utterson] dozed over," the author writes, "it was but to see [Hyde] glide more stealthily through sleeping houses, or move the more swiftly ... through wider labyrinths of lamp-lighted city, and at every street corner crush a child and leave her screaming." In Utterson's dreams, then, Hyde appears ubiquitous, permeating the city with his dark nature and his crimes. This idea of Hyde as a universal presence suggests that this faceless figure, crushing children and standing by Jekyll's bed, symbolizes all the secret sins that lurk beneath the surface of respectable London. This notion of hidden crimes recurs throughout the novel. It is significant that Stevenson never gives us any details of Jekyll's indiscretions prior to his creation of Hyde, nor of Hyde's wicked, dissipated habits. The crimes remain shrouded in mystery; to explain them in rational language would strip them of their supernatural and eerie quality.

Hyde's ugliness prompts a similar loss of words. When Utterson finally converses with Hyde and sees his face, like Enfield, he proves unable to comprehend and delineate exactly what makes Hyde so ugly and frightening. Significantly, though, one of the words that the fumbling lawyer comes up with is "troglodyte," a term referring to a prehistoric, manlike creature. Through this word, the text links the immoral Hyde to the notion of recidivism—a fall from civilization and a regression to a more primitive state. The imperialist age of Victorian England manifested a great fear of recidivism, particularly in its theories of racial science, in which theorists cautioned that lesser, savage peoples might swallow up the supposedly superior white races.

The description of Jekyll's house introduces an element of clear symbolism. The doctor lives in a well-appointed home, described by Stevenson as having "a great air of wealth and comfort." The building secretly connects to his laboratory, which faces out on another street and appears sinister and run-down. It is in the laboratory that Dr. Jekyll becomes Mr. Hyde. Like the two secretly connected buildings, seemingly having nothing to do with each other but in fact easily traversed, the upstanding Jekyll and the corrupt Hyde appear separate but in fact share an unseen inner connection.

These chapters also introduce us to the minor character of Dr. Lanyon, Jekyll's former colleague. Lanyon's labeling of Jekyll's research as "unscientific balderdash" hints at the supernatural bent of the experiments, which contrasts powerfully with the prevailing scientific consensus of the Victorian world, in which rationalism and materialism held sway. In his reverence for the rational and logical, Lanyon emerges as the quintessential nineteenth-century scientist, automatically dismissing Jekyll's mystical experiments. Later events prove that his dogmatic faith in a purely material science is more akin to superstition than Jekyll's experiments.

CHAPTERS 4–5

SUMMARY — CHAPTER 4: "THE CAREW MURDER CASE"

Approximately one year later, the scene opens on a maid who, sitting at her window in the wee hours of the morning, witnesses a murder take place in the street below. She sees a small, evil-looking man, whom she recognizes as Mr. Hyde, encounter a polite, aged gentleman; when the gentleman offers Hyde a greeting, Hyde suddenly turns on him with a stick, beating him to death. The police find a letter addressed to Utterson on the dead body, and they consequently summon the lawyer. He identifies the body as Sir Danvers Carew, a popular member of Parliament and one of his clients.

Utterson still has Hyde's address, and he accompanies the police to a set of rooms located in a poor, evil-looking part of town. Utterson reflects on how odd it is that a man who lives in such squalor is the heir to Henry Jekyll's fortune. Hyde's villainous-looking landlady lets the men in, but the suspected murderer is not at home. The police find the murder weapon and the burned remains of Hyde's checkbook. Upon a subsequent visit to the bank, the police inspector learns that Hyde still has an account there. The officer assumes that he need only wait for Hyde to go and withdraw money. In the days and weeks that follow, however, no sign of Hyde turns up; he has no family, no friends, and those who have seen him are unable to give accurate descriptions, differ on details, and agree only on the evil aspect of his appearance.

SUMMARY — CHAPTER 5: "INCIDENT OF THE LETTER"

Utterson calls on Jekyll, whom he finds in his laboratory looking deathly ill. Jekyll feverishly claims that Hyde has left and that their relationship has ended. He also assures Utterson that the police shall never find the man. Jekyll then shows Utterson a letter and asks him what he should do with it, since he fears it could damage his reputation if he turns it over to the police. The letter is from Hyde, assuring

Jekyll that he has means of escape, that Jekyll should not worry about him, and that he deems himself unworthy of Jekyll's great generosity. Utterson asks if Hyde dictated the terms of Jekyll's will—especially its insistence that Hyde inherit in the event of Jekyll's "disappearance." Jekyll replies in the affirmative, and Utterson tells his friend that Hyde probably meant to murder him and that he has had a near escape. He takes the letter and departs.

On his way out, Utterson runs into Poole, the butler, and asks him to describe the man who delivered the letter; Poole, taken aback, claims to have no knowledge of any letters being delivered other than the usual mail. That night, over drinks, Utterson consults his trusted clerk, Mr. Guest, who is an expert on handwriting. Guest compares Hyde's letter with some of Jekyll's own writing and suggests that the same hand inscribed both; Hyde's script merely leans in the opposite direction, as if for the purpose of concealment. Utterson reacts with alarm at the thought that Jekyll would forge a letter for a murderer.

ANALYSIS — CHAPTERS 4–5

Chapter 4 illustrates the extent of Hyde's capacity for evil. Whereas we might earlier take Hyde for nothing more than an unscrupulous opportunist, manipulating Jekyll, the mindlessly vicious nature of the man becomes clear with the violent murder of Sir Danvers Carew. Hyde is violent at random, with no apparent motive, and with little concern for his own safety—as his willingness to beat a man to death in the middle of a public street demonstrates. His complete disappearance after the murder, along with his utter lack of family, friends, and people who can identify him, suggests that he possesses some kind of otherworldly origin.

In Chapter 5, as in the rest of the novel, Utterson staunchly remains the proper Victorian gentleman, despite the disturbing nature of the events that he investigates. Even as he plays the detective, his principal desire remains the avoidance of scandal rather than the discovery of truth. Thus, even when he suspects Jekyll of covering up for a murderer, he reports nothing of it to anyone, preferring to set the matter aside in the hopes of preserving his client's reputation. Utterson's insistence on propriety and the maintenance of appearances deeply hinders his ability to learn the truth about Jekyll and Hyde. Moreover, this insistence reflects a shortcoming in the Victorian society that the lawyer represents. Stevenson suggests that society focuses so exclusively on outward appearances and respectability that it remains blind to the fact that human beings also possess a darker side, replete with malevolent instincts and irrational passions. Society, like Utterson, cannot see that a seemingly upstanding person can also possess an evil potential hidden within.

Yet, despite Utterson's straitlaced and unimaginative perspective on the mystery, the eerie aura of the situation reaches such intensity as to effect even this reserved gentleman. Earlier, Utterson has dreams in which London is transformed into a nightmare landscape through which Hyde stalks, committing violence against innocents. The image of the city as a place of hidden terrors recurs, but this time Utterson is awake and driving with the police to Hyde's rooms in the early morning. A fog has gripped London, and it swirls and eddies through the gloomy neighborhoods, making them seem "like a district of some city in a nightmare." As in all of his portrayals of London, Stevenson lavishes his descriptive skill on the passage, rendering the depicted landscape as a nest of hidden wickedness. Here, he describes the "great chocolate-coloured pall lowered over heaven ... here it would be dark like the back-end of evening; and there would be a glow of a rich, lurid brown ... and here ... a haggard shaft of daylight would glance in between the swirling wreaths." It is important to note, however, that Stevenson attributes these poetic descriptions to Utterson. The words may seem out of character for the rather unimaginative lawyer, but one could also interpret them as testifying to the power of Hyde's horror. Perhaps the disturbing nature of Hyde's behavior and his residence bring out a darker side in Utterson himself, one in touch with the supernatural terrors lurking behind the facade of the everyday world.

The above passage offers an excellent example of Stevenson's ability to use evocative language to establish a sense of the uncanny in a narrative that is otherwise dry and forthright. Much of *Dr. Jekyll and Mr. Hyde* is written in a brisk, businesslike, and factual way, like a police report on a strange affair rather than a novel. This tone derives from the personality of Mr. Utterson but also seems to arise from the text itself. The original title, *The Strange Case of Dr. Jekyll and Mr. Hyde,* and chapter headings such as "Incident of the Letter" and "Incident at the Window" contribute to this reserved, dispassionate tone, as if detectives themselves have been titling each report for a ledger. But in passages like the one above, Stevenson injects rich, evocative descriptions into the narrative. This richer language performs a duty that Stevenson's placid characterization of Utterson does not; more important, it creates a link between the language of the text and the actions of the characters. The author thus not only hints at a darker side within Utterson but also at a darker side within the text itself, which typically keeps up appearances as a logical and linear narrative but periodically sinks into decadent flourishes. Utterson and the text, then, become metaphors for humanity in general, and for society at large, both of which may appear logically oriented and straightforward but, in fact, contain darker undercurrents.

CHAPTERS 6–7

SUMMARY — CHAPTER 6: "REMARKABLE INCIDENT OF DR. LANYON"

As time passes, with no sign of Hyde's reappearance, Jekyll becomes healthier-looking and more sociable, devoting himself to charity. To Utterson, it appears that the removal of Hyde's evil influence has had a tremendously positive effect on Jekyll. After two months of this placid lifestyle, Jekyll holds a dinner party, which both Utterson and Lanyon attend, and the three talk together as old friends. But a few days later, when Utterson calls on Jekyll, Poole reports that his master is receiving no visitors.

This scenario repeats itself for a week, so Utterson goes to visit Lanyon, hoping to learn why Jekyll has refused any company. He finds Lanyon in very poor health, pale and sickly, with a frightened look in his eyes. Lanyon explains that he has had a great shock and expects to die in a few weeks. "[L]ife has been pleasant," he says. "I liked it; yes, sir, I used to like it." Then he adds, "I sometimes think if we knew all, we should be more glad to get away." When Utterson mentions that Jekyll also seems ill, Lanyon violently demands that they talk of anything but Jekyll. He promises that after his death, Utterson may learn the truth about everything, but for now he will not discuss it. Afterward, at home, Utterson writes to Jekyll, talking about being turned away from Jekyll's house and inquiring as to what caused the break between him and Lanyon. Soon Jekyll's written reply arrives, explaining that while he still cares for Lanyon, he understands why the doctor says they must not meet. As for Jekyll himself, he pledges his continued affection for Utterson but adds that from now on he will be maintaining a strict seclusion, seeing no one. He says that he is suffering a punishment that he cannot name.

Lanyon dies a few weeks later, fulfilling his prophecy. After the funeral, Utterson takes from his safe a letter that Lanyon meant for him to read after he died. Inside, Utterson finds only another envelope, marked to remain sealed until Jekyll also has died. Out of professional principle, Utterson overcomes his curiosity and puts the envelope away for safekeeping. As weeks pass, he calls on Jekyll less and less frequently, and the butler continues to refuse him entry.

SUMMARY — CHAPTER 7: "INCIDENT AT THE WINDOW"
The following Sunday, Utterson and Enfield are taking their regular stroll. Passing the door where Enfield once saw Hyde enter to retrieve Jekyll's check, Enfield remarks on the murder case. He notes that the story that began with the trampling has reached an end, as London will never again see Mr. Hyde. Enfield mentions that in the intervening weeks he has learned that the run-down laboratory they pass is physically connected to Jekyll's house, and they both stop to peer into the house's windows, with Utterson noting his concern for Jekyll's health. To their surprise, the two men find Jekyll at the window, enjoying the fresh air. Jekyll complains that he feels "very low," and Utterson suggests that he join them for a walk, to help his circulation. Jekyll refuses, saying that he cannot go out. Then, just as they resume polite conversation, a look of terror seizes his face, and he quickly shuts the window and vanishes. Utterson and Enfield depart in shocked silence.

ANALYSIS — CHAPTERS 6–7
By this point in the story, it becomes clear that the mystery of Jekyll's relationship to Hyde has proven too much for Utterson's rational approach and search for logical explanations. The uncanny aspects of Hyde's appearance, behavior, and ability to disappear should suffice to indicate the fantastical air of the situation. At this point, however, the strange tragedy surrounding Lanyon roots the mystery in distinctly supernatural territory. Until this point, Lanyon's main significance to the story has been his function as a representative of reason. He dismisses Jekyll's experiments as "unscientific balderdash" and embodies the rational man of science, in distinct opposition to superstition and fantasy. Ironically, all of Lanyon's earlier sentiments seem to have given way to a cryptic, unexplained horror. Lanyon's deterioration mirrors the gradual erosion of logic in the face of the supernatural in the novel.

SUMMARY & ANALYSIS

This erosion is accompanied by a further breakdown of language. As we see earlier, *Dr. Jekyll and Mr. Hyde* seems to present language—a rational, logical mode of perceiving and containing the world—as existing in opposition to the fanciful or fantastical. For example, Stevenson refrains from describing Hyde's crimes or Jekyll's youthful debaucheries in detail, as if such explanations might reduce the haunting effect of these wicked actions. Correspondingly, just as language might break down and defuse an aura of the uncanny, the uncanny can prompt a breakdown in language. Hyde's ugliness instigates one such loss of words. As we have seen, when Enfield and Utterson see Hyde's face, they prove unable to describe what exactly makes Hyde so ugly and frightening.

But the novel is permeated by other silences as well, more akin to refusals than failures to speak: Lanyon refuses to describe to Utterson what he has seen; Jekyll declines to discuss his relationship with Hyde; after witnessing Jekyll's strange disappearance from the window, Utterson and Enfield say almost nothing about it; and Utterson carries out an informal investigation of Hyde and Jekyll but never mentions his suspicions to anyone. This second set of silences derives not so much from being involuntarily awestruck by the uncanny, but rather points to an acknowledgment of a situation that exceeds the boundaries of logic, yet with an unwillingness to pursue it further or express it openly. Such unwillingness seems to stem, in turn, from a concern for reputation and public morality. Significantly, both Jekyll and Lanyon leave written records of what they have seen and done but insist that these records not be opened until after their deaths. In other words, the truth can be exposed only after the death of the person whose reputation it might ruin. Stevenson may suggest that such refusals to discuss the grittier side of life mirror a similar tendency in Victorian society at large.

CHAPTER 8: "THE LAST NIGHT"

SUMMARY

Jekyll's butler Poole visits Utterson one night after dinner. Deeply agitated, he says only that he believes there has been some "foul play" regarding Dr. Jekyll; he quickly brings Utterson to his master's residence. The night is dark and windy, and the streets are deserted, giving Utterson a premonition of disaster. When he reaches Jekyll's house, he finds the servants gathered fearfully in the main hall. Poole brings Utterson to the door of Jekyll's laboratory and calls inside, saying that Utterson has come for a visit. A strange voice responds, sounding nothing like that of Jekyll; the owner of the voice tells Poole that he can receive no visitors.

Poole and Utterson retreat to the kitchen, where Poole insists that the voice they heard emanating from the laboratory does not belong to his master. Utterson wonders why the murderer would remain in the laboratory if he had just killed Jekyll and not simply flee. Poole describes how the mystery voice has sent him on constant errands to chemists; the man in the laboratory seems desperate for some ingredient that no drugstore in London sells. Utterson, still hopeful, asks whether the notes Poole has received are in the doctor's hand, but Poole then reveals that he has seen the person inside the laboratory, when he came out briefly to search for something, and that the man looked nothing like Jekyll. Utterson suggests that Jekyll may have some disease that changes his voice and deforms his features, making them unrecognizable, but Poole declares that the person he saw was smaller than his master—and looked, in fact, like none other than Mr. Hyde.

Hearing Poole's words, Utterson resolves that he and Poole should break into the laboratory. He sends two servants around the block the laboratory's other door, the one that Enfield sees Hyde using at the beginning of the novel. Then, armed with a fireplace poker and an axe, Utterson and Poole return to the inner door. Utterson calls inside, demanding admittance. The voice begs for Utterson to have mercy and to leave him alone. The lawyer, however, recognizes the voice as Hyde's and orders Poole to smash down the door.

Once inside, the men find Hyde's body lying on the floor, a crushed vial in his hand. He appears to have poisoned himself. Utterson notes that Hyde is wearing a suit that belongs to Jekyll and that is much too large for him. The men search the entire laboratory, as well as the surgeon's theater below and the other rooms in the building, but they find neither a trace of Jekyll nor a corpse. They note a large mirror and think it strange to find such an item in a scientific laboratory. Then, on Jekyll's business table, they find a large envelope addressed to Utterson that contains three items. The first is a will, much like the previous one, except that it replaces Hyde's name with Utterson's. The second is a note to Utterson, with the present day's date on it. Based on this piece of evidence, Utterson surmises that Jekyll is still alive—and he wonders if Hyde really died by suicide or if Jekyll killed him. This note instructs Utterson to go home immediately and read the letter that Lanyon gave him earlier. It adds that if he desires to learn more, Utterson can read the confession of "Your worthy and unhappy friend, Henry Jekyll." Utterson takes the third item from the envelope—a sealed packet—and promises Poole that he will return that night and send for the police. He then heads back to his office to read Lanyon's letter and the contents of the sealed packet.

ANALYSIS

In the classic detective story, this climactic chapter would contain the scene in which the detective, having solved the case, reveals his ingenious solution and fingers the culprit. But, in spite of Utterson's efforts in investigating the matter of Jekyll and Hyde, he has made no progress in solving the mystery. Indeed, were it not for the existence of Lanyon's letter and Jekyll's confession, which make up the last two chapters, it seems likely that the truth about Jekyll and Hyde never would be ascertained.

One cannot blame Utterson for failing to solve the case of Jekyll and Hyde before reading the letters—even the most skilled professional detective could not have deduced the supernatural circumstances surrounding the doctor and his darker half. Nevertheless, Stevenson uses this chapter to emphasize just how far away from the truth Utterson remains, extending almost to the point of absurdity. The servants, led by Poole, remain more in touch with the reality of the situation; they *know* that something terrible has happened to their master, and so they forsake their duties and huddle together out of fright. Upon seeing them gathered in fear, Utterson reacts with a response characteristic of his all-consuming concern for propriety and the upkeep of appearances. Instead of looking for the cause of the servants' terror, he is more concerned with maintaining decorum and social hierarchy. "What, what?" he bursts out. "Are you all here? . . . Very irregular, very unseemly; your master would be far from pleased."

Even at this time of clear crisis, Utterson is unwilling to allow for any breach of propriety and order. As he talks with Poole before the locked door of the laboratory, Utterson is growing desperate to avoid taking action. He offers more and more absurd explanations for what Poole has seen that culminate in his suggestion that Jekyll has a disease that has changed his appearance to the point of unrecognizability. Utterson is willing to accept any explanation, however improbable, before doing anything so indecorous as breaking down a door. Moreover, his unwillingness to break into Jekyll's laboratory reflects his continued concern for his friend's reputation. As long as he does not break in, he seems to think, Jekyll's good name will be preserved. In portraying Utterson's absurd mind-set, Stevenson seems to comment on the larger Victorian mentality and on what one might see as its privileging of order and decorum over truth.

But Utterson's unwillingness to penetrate the mystery of his friend's situation is more than the expression of his Victorian desire to avoid scandal. He seems to have a premonition that what awaits him in the laboratory constitutes not merely a breach of order but the toppling of one order by another. His conversation with Poole is a frantic attempt to avoid entering the world of supernatural terrors that Jekyll has loosed.

It is this sense of supernatural terror breaking into everyday reality that places *Dr. Jekyll and Mr. Hyde* firmly within the tradition of Gothic fiction, which flourished in nineteenth-century Europe—and particularly in Britain, where such Gothic masterpieces as *Dracula, The Turn of the Screw, Frankenstein,* and *Jane Eyre* were penned. The term "Gothic" covers a wide variety of stories, but certain recurring themes and motifs define the genre. Gothic tales may contain explicitly supernatural material, as *Dracula* does, or imply supernatural phenomena without narrating it directly, as *Jekyll and Hyde* does. They may not allude to supernatural events at all, but simply convey a sense of the uncanny, of dark and disturbing elements that break into the routine of prosaic, everyday life, as *Jane Eyre* does. Gothic novels often center around secrets—such as Jekyll's connection to Hyde—or around doppelgängers, a German term referring to people who resemble other characters in strange, disconcerting ways. Frankenstein's monster is a doppelgänger for Frankenstein, just as Hyde is for Jekyll. Above all, Gothic novels depend upon geography for their power. Nearly every Gothic novel takes place in some strange, eerie locale from which the characters have difficulty escaping, be it Dracula's castle, the estate of Thornfield in *Jane Eyre,* or the decaying homes and palaces that appear in the stories of the greatest practitioner of American Gothic fiction, Edgar Allan Poe. In *Dr. Jekyll and Mr. Hyde,* of course, that uncanny place is the fog-blanketed world of nighttime London.

Although the dialogue in this chapter arguably interrupts the dramatic momentum of the situation, Stevenson nevertheless conjures a mood of dread, primarily through the use of evocative language. For example, as Poole and Utterson stand ready to break down the door, the text declares that "[t]he scud had banked over the moon, and it was now quite dark. The wind, which only broke in puffs and draughts into that deep well of building, tossed the light of the candle to and fro about their steps." And earlier, as Utterson and Poole travel through the empty streets to reach Jekyll's home, Stevenson revisits his frequent image of London as a nightmare city, where darkness—both moral and physical—holds sway.

CHAPTER 9: "DR. LANYON'S NARRATIVE"

SUMMARY

> *He put the glass to his lips, and drank at one gulp. . . .*
> *there before my eyes . . . there stood Henry Jekyll!*
> (See QUOTATIONS, p. 45)

This chapter constitutes a word-for-word transcription of the letter Lanyon intends Utterson to open after Lanyon's and Jekyll's deaths. Lanyon writes that after Jekyll's last dinner party, he received a strange letter from Jekyll. The letter asked Lanyon to go to Jekyll's home and, with the help of Poole, break into the upper room—or "cabinet"—of Jekyll's laboratory. The letter instructed Lanyon then to remove a specific drawer and all its contents from the laboratory, return with this drawer to his own home, and wait for a man who would come to claim it precisely at midnight. The letter seemed to Lanyon to have been written in a mood of desperation. It offered no explanation for the orders it gave but promised Lanyon that if he did as it bade, he would soon understand everything.

Lanyon duly went to Jekyll's home, where Poole and a locksmith met him. The locksmith broke into the lab, and Lanyon returned home with the drawer. Within the drawer, Lanyon found several vials, one containing what seemed to be salt and another holding a peculiar red liquid. The drawer also contained a notebook recording what seemed to be years of experiments, with little notations such as "double" or "total failure!!!" scattered amid a long list of dates. However, the notebooks offered no hints as to what the experiments involved. Lanyon waited for his visitor, increasingly certain that Jekyll must be insane. As promised, at the stroke of midnight, a small, evil-looking man appeared, dressed in clothes much too large for him. It was, of course, Mr. Hyde, but Lanyon, never having seen the man before, did not recognize him. Hyde seemed nervous and excited. He avoided polite conversation, interested only in the contents of the drawer. Lanyon directed him to it, and Hyde then asked for a graduated glass. In it, he mixed the ingredients from the drawer to form a purple liquid, which then became green. Hyde paused and asked Lanyon whether he should leave and take the glass with him, or whether he should stay and drink it in front of Lanyon, allowing the doctor to witness something that he claimed would "stagger the unbelief of Satan." Lanyon, irritated, declared that he had already become so involved in the matter that he wanted to see the end of it.

Taking up the glass, Hyde told Lanyon that his skepticism of "transcendental medicine" would now be disproved. Before Lanyon's eyes, the deformed man drank the glass in one gulp and then seemed to swell, his body expanding, his face melting and shifting, until, shockingly, Hyde was gone and Dr. Jekyll stood in his place. Lanyon here ends his letter, stating that what Jekyll told him afterward is too shocking to repeat and that the horror of the event has so wrecked his constitution that he will soon die.

———————————

ANALYSIS

This chapter finally makes explicit the nature of Dr. Jekyll's relationship to his darker half, Mr. Hyde—the men are one and the same person. Lanyon's narrative offers a smaller mystery within the larger mystery of the novel: the doctor is presented with a puzzling set of instructions from his friend Jekyll without any explanation of what the instructions mean. We know more than Lanyon, of course, and instantly realize that the small man who strikes Lanyon with a "disgustful curiosity" can be none other than Hyde. But even this knowledge does not diminish the shocking effect of the climax of the novel, the moment when we finally witness the interchange between the two identities. Through the astonished eyes of Lanyon, Stevenson offers a vivid description, using detailed language and imagery to lend immediacy to supernatural events.

Yet it is worth noting that for all the details that the doctor's account includes, this chapter offers very little *explanation* of what Lanyon sees. We learn that Hyde and Jekyll are the same person and that the two personas can morph into one another with the help of a mysterious potion. We remain largely in the dark, however, as to how or why this situation came about. Lanyon states that Jekyll told him everything after the transformation was complete, but he refrains from telling Utterson, declaring that "[w]hat he told me in the next hour I cannot bring my mind to set on paper."

As with previous silences in the novel, this silence owes to a character's refusal to confront truths that upset his worldview. As we have seen in previous chapters, Jekyll has delved into mystical investigations of the nature of man, whereas Lanyon has adhered strictly to rational, materialist science. Indeed, in some sense, Lanyon cannot conceive of the world that Jekyll has entered; thus, when he is forced to confront this world as manifested in Hyde's transformation, he retreats deep within himself, spurning this phenomenon that shatters his worldview. The impact of the shock is such that it causes Lanyon, a scientist committed to pursuing knowledge, to declare in Chapter 6, "I sometimes think if we knew all, we should be more glad to get away." Lanyon has decided that some knowledge is not worth the cost of obtaining or possessing it. Like Utterson and Enfield, he prefers silence to the exposure of dark truths. The task of exposing these truths must fall to Henry Jekyll himself, in the final chapter of the novel. As the only character to have embraced the darker side of the world, Jekyll remains the only one willing to speak of it.

SUMMARY & ANALYSIS

CHAPTER 10: "HENRY JEKYLL'S FULL STATEMENT OF THE CASE"

SUMMARY

> *I learned to recognise the thorough and primitive*
> *duality of man . . . if I could rightly be said to be*
> *either, it was only because I was radically both.*
> (See QUOTATIONS, p. 46)

This chapter offers a transcription of the letter Jekyll leaves for Utterson in the laboratory. Jekyll writes that upon his birth he possessed a large inheritance, a healthy body, and a hardworking, decent nature. His idealism allowed him to maintain a respectable seriousness in public while hiding his more frivolous and indecent side. By the time he was fully grown, he found himself leading a dual life, in which his better side constantly felt guilt for the transgressions of his darker side. When his scientific interests led to mystical studies as to the divided nature of man, he hoped to find some solution to his own split nature. Jekyll insists that "man is not truly one, but truly two," and he records how he dreamed of separating the good and evil natures.

Jekyll reports that, after much research, he eventually found a chemical solution that might serve his purposes. Buying a large quantity of salt as his last ingredient, he took the potion with the knowledge that he was risking his life, but he remained driven by the hopes of making a great discovery. At first, he experienced incredible pain and nausea. But as these symptoms subsided, he felt vigorous and filled with recklessness and sensuality. He had become the shrunken, deformed Mr. Hyde. He hypothesizes that Hyde's small stature owed to the fact that this persona represented his evil side alone, which up to that point had been repressed.

Upon first looking into a mirror after the transformation, Jekyll-turned-Hyde was not repulsed by his new form; instead, he experienced "a leap of welcome." He came to delight in living as Hyde. Jekyll was becoming too old to act upon his more embarrassing impulses, but Hyde was a younger man, the personification of the evil side that emerged several years after Jekyll's own birth. Transforming himself into Hyde became a welcome outlet for Jekyll's passions. Jekyll furnished a home and set up a bank account for his alter ego, Hyde, who soon sunk into utter degradation. But each time he transformed back into Jekyll, he felt no guilt at Hyde's dark exploits, though he did try to right whatever wrongs had been done.

It was not until two months before the Carew murder that Jekyll found cause for concern. While asleep one night, he involuntarily transformed into Hyde—without the help of the potion—and awoke in the body of his darker half. This incident convinced him that he must cease with his transformations or risk being trapped in Hyde's form forever. But after two months as Jekyll, he caved in and took the potion again. Hyde, so long repressed, emerged wild and vengefully savage, and it was in this mood that he beat Carew to death, delighting in the crime. Hyde showed no remorse for the murder, but Jekyll knelt and prayed to God for forgiveness even before his transformation back was complete. The horrifying nature of the murder convinced Jekyll never to transform himself again, and it was during the subsequent months that Utterson and others remarked that Jekyll seemed to have had a weight lifted from his shoulders, and that everything seemed well with him.

Eventually, though, Jekyll grew weary of constant virtue and indulged some of his darker desires—in his own person, not that of Hyde. But this dip into darkness proved sufficient to cause another spontaneous transformation into Hyde, which took place one day when Jekyll was sitting in a park, far from home. As Hyde, he immediately felt brave and powerful, but he also knew that the police would seize him for his murder of Carew. He could not even return to his rooms to get his potions without a great risk of being captured. It was then that he sent word to Lanyon to break into his laboratory and get his potions for him. After that night, he had to take a double dose of the potion every six hours to avoid spontaneous transformation into Hyde. As soon as the drug began to wear off, the transformation process would begin. It was one of these spells that struck him as he spoke to Enfield and Utterson out the window, forcing him to withdraw.

In his last, desperate hours, Hyde grew stronger as Jekyll grew weaker. Moreover, the salt necessary for the potion began to run out. Jekyll ordered more, only to discover that the mineral did not have the same effect; he realized that the original salt must have contained an impurity that made the potion work. Jekyll then anticipated the fast approach of the moment when he must become Hyde permanently. He thus used the last of the potion to buy himself time during which to compose this final letter. Jekyll writes that he does not know whether, when faced with discovery, Hyde will kill himself or be arrested and hanged—but he knows that by the time Utterson reads this letter, Henry Jekyll will be no more.

> *[As] the first edge of my penitence wore off ... a qualm came over me, a horrid nausea and the most deadly shuddering.* (See QUOTATIONS, p. 47)

ANALYSIS

At this point all the mysteries of the novel unravel, as we encounter a second account of the same events that have been unfolding throughout the novel. Only this time, instead of seeing them from the point of view of Utterson, we see them from the point of view of Jekyll—and, by extension, that of Hyde. This shift in point of view makes a great difference indeed. All the events that seemed puzzling or inexplicable before are suddenly explained: Jekyll's confession makes clear the will that left everything to Hyde; it tells of the events leading up to the brutal murder of Carew; it clarifies the mystery of the similarity between Jekyll's and Hyde's handwritings; it elucidates why Jekyll seemed to improve dramatically after Carew's murder, and why he abruptly went into a decline and was forced into seclusion. We know, finally, the details behind Hyde's midnight visit to Lanyon and Jekyll's bizarre disappearance from the window while talking to Enfield and Utterson; so, too, is Jekyll's final disappearance explained. It is as if there have been two parallel narratives throughout the novel, and we have, until now, been given access only to one. With Jekyll's confession, however, everything falls into place.

Jekyll's meditations on the dual nature of man, which prompt his forays into the experiments that bring forth Hyde, point to the novel's central question about the nature of the relationship between the good and evil portions of the human soul. As the embodiment of the dark side of man, Hyde is driven by passion and heedless of moral constraints. Yet it is important to note that while Hyde exists as distilled evil, Jekyll remains a mixture of good and evil. Jekyll repeatedly claims that his goal was to liberate his light half from his darker impulses, yet the opposite seems to happen. His dark side is given flesh, while his better half is not. Moreover, his dark side grows ever stronger as the novel continues, until the old, half-good and half-evil Jekyll ceases to exist.

Hyde is smaller than Jekyll, and younger, which leads Jekyll to surmise that his evil part is smaller and less developed than his good part. Yet Hyde's physical strength might suggest the opposite—that the evil side possesses a superior power and vigor. Jekyll's initial delight whenever he becomes Hyde seems to support this viewpoint, as does the fact that, no matter how appalling the crimes Hyde commits, Jekyll never feels guilty enough to refrain from making the transformation again as soon as he feels the urge. "Henry Jekyll stood at times aghast before the acts of Edward Hyde," Jekyll writes, "but the situation was apart from ordinary laws, and insidiously relaxed the grasp of conscience. It was Hyde, after all, and Hyde alone, that was guilty." But such statements seem little more than an absurd attempt at self-justification. For it is Jekyll who brings Hyde into being, clearly knowing that he embodies pure evil. Jekyll therefore bears responsibility for Hyde's actions. Indeed, his willingness to convince himself otherwise suggests, again, that the darker half of the man has the upper hand, even when he is Jekyll and not Hyde.

With these pieces of evidence, Stevenson suggests the immensity of humanity's dark impulses, which conscience can barely hold in check. In the end, then, although he portrays Utterson and Enfield as somewhat absurd in their denial of evil, Stevenson also may sympathize with their determination to repress their dark sides completely. Evil may be so strong that such strategies offer the only possibility for order and morality in society. The alternative—actively exploring the darkness—leads one into the trap that closes permanently on the hapless Jekyll, whose conscientious, civilized self proves no match for the violence unleashed in the person of Hyde.

Interestingly, even in this confessional chapter, certain details of the story's horrors remain obscure. Jekyll refuses to give any description of his youthful sins, and he does not actually elaborate on any of the "depravity"— except the murder of Carew—in which Hyde engages. As with other silences in the book, this absence of explanation may point to the clash between rational articulation and the irrationality of profound evil. Perhaps these deeds are so depraved that they defy all attempts at true explanation, or perhaps Stevenson fears that to describe them explicitly would be to destroy their eerie power.

But in this chapter in particular, the silence may also indicate not a failure of words but, as in other instances, a refusal to use them. Earlier in the novel, reserved and decorous men such as Enfield and

Utterson, wanting to deny the darker elements of humanity, make such a refusal. Here, however, one can hardly ascribe the silences to a character's denial of evil, since the letter that constitutes this chapter comes from Jekyll himself. The absence of description may owe not to any repression within the novel itself but to the repressive tendencies of the world in which Stevenson wrote. Rigid Victorian norms would not have allowed him to elaborate upon Jekyll's and Hyde's crimes if they were tremendously gruesome; Stevenson thus discusses them in a vague (and thus acceptable) mannter.

While Victorian society forbade the discussion of many issues, sexuality stood at the top of the blacklist. Based on other indications in the novel, one can reasonably infer that the misdeeds of Jekyll and Hyde are sexual in nature. For example, upon the novel's introduction of Hyde, Hyde tramples a young girl underfoot and then pays off her family. Child prostitution was rampant in Victorian London, and there may be a suggestion of it here. Moreover, in a novel whose characters are all staunch bachelors, one might interpret the "depravity" mentioned in the text as acts of hidden homosexuality. Late Victorian literature contains many subtle allusions to covert acts of socially unaccepted sexual behavior, often referring to or symbolizing homosexual activities. Oscar Wilde's novel *The Picture of Dorian Gray* provides an excellent example of Victorian literature's concern and anxiety regarding sexual orientation.

In the end, though, the actual nature of Hyde's and Jekyll's sins proves less important than Stevenson's larger point, which is that the lure of the dark side constitutes a universal part of our human nature. We are all Jekylls, desperately trying to keep our Hydes under control—even as we are secretly fascinated by what they do and envious of their frightening freedom from moral constraints.

SUMMARY & ANALYSIS

Important Quotations Explained

1. Mr. Utterson the lawyer was a man of a rugged countenance, that was never lighted by a smile; cold, scanty and embarrassed in discourse; backward in sentiment; lean, long, dusty, dreary, and yet somehow lovable. . . . He was austere with himself; drank gin when he was alone, to mortify a taste for vintages; and though he enjoyed the theater, had not crossed the doors of one for twenty years. But he had an approved tolerance for others; sometimes wondering, almost with envy, at the high pressure of spirits involved in their misdeeds; and in any extremity inclined to help rather than to reprove. . . . [I]t was frequently his fortune to be the last reputable acquaintance and the last good influence in the lives of down-going men.

This passage is taken from the first paragraph of the novel, in which Stevenson sketches the character of Utterson the lawyer, through whose eyes the bulk of the novel unfolds. In a sense, Utterson comes across as an uninteresting character—unsmiling, "scanty" in speech, "lean, long, dusty, dreary" in person. As we know from later passages in the novel, he never stoops to gossip and struggles to maintain propriety even to the point of absurdity; the above passage notes the man's "auster[ity]."

Yet this introductory passage also reveals certain cracks in this rigid, civilized facade—cracks that make Utterson an ideal person to pursue the bizarre case of Jekyll and Hyde. For one thing, the passage draws attention to Utterson's "lovab[ility]," his tendency to "help rather than to reprove." This geniality and approachability positions Utterson at the center of the novel's social web—all of the other characters confide in him and turn to him for help, allowing him glimpses of the mystery from every point of view. Both Lanyon and Jekyll confide in him; his friendship with Enfield gives him a salient piece of information early in the novel; Poole comes to him when Jekyll's situation reaches a crisis point. Utterson even serves as the attorney for Sir Danvers Carew, Hyde's victim. Second, the passage notes Utterson's keen interest in individuals with dark secrets, in those who suffer from scandal. Indeed, the text observes, Utterson sometimes wonders with near "envy" at the motivations behind people's wrongdoings or missteps. It is this curiosity, seemingly out of place in a dully respectable man, that prompts him to involve himself in the unfolding mystery.

2.   "He is not easy to describe. There is something wrong with his appearance; something displeasing, something downright detestable. I never saw a man I so disliked, and yet I scarce know why. He must be deformed somewhere; he gives a strong feeling of deformity, although I couldn't specify the point. He's an extraordinary-looking man, and yet I really can name nothing out of the way. No, sir; I can make no hand of it; I can't describe him. And it's not want of memory; for I declare I can see him this moment."

This quotation appears in Chapter 1, "Story of the Door," when Enfield relates to Utterson how he watched Hyde trample a little girl underfoot. Utterson asks his friend to describe Hyde's appearance, but Enfield, as the quote indicates, proves unable to formulate a clear portrait. He asserts that Hyde is deformed, ugly, and inspires an immediate revulsion, yet he cannot say why.

Enfield's lack of eloquence sets a pattern for the novel, as no one—from Utterson himself to witnesses describing Hyde to the police—can come up with an exact description of the man. Most people merely conclude that he appears ugly and deformed in some indefinable way. These failures of articulation create an impression of Hyde as an uncanny figure, someone whose deformity is truly intangible, mysterious, perceptible only with some sort of sixth sense for which no vocabulary exists. It is almost as if language itself fails when it tries to come to grips with Hyde; he is beyond words, just as he is beyond morality and conscience. As a supernatural creation, he does not quite belong in the world; correspondingly, he evades the conceptual faculties of normal human beings.

3. He put the glass to his lips, and drank at one gulp. A cry followed; he reeled, staggered, clutched at the table and held on, staring with injected eyes, gasping with open mouth; and as I looked there came, I thought, a change—he seemed to swell—his face became suddenly black and the features seemed to melt and alter—and at the next moment, I had sprung to my feet and leaped back against the wall, my arm raised to shield me from that prodigy, my mind submerged in terror.

    "O God!" I screamed, and "O God!" again and again; for there before my eyes—pale and shaken, and half fainting, and groping before him with his hands, like a man restored from death—there stood Henry Jekyll!

This quotation appears in Chapter 9, "Dr. Lanyon's Narrative," as Lanyon describes the moment when Hyde, drinking the potion whose ingredients Lanyon procured from Jekyll's laboratory, transforms himself back into Jekyll. Lanyon, who earlier ridicules Jekyll's experiments as "unscientific balderdash," now sees the proof of Jekyll's success. The sight so horrifies him that he dies shortly after this scene. The transformation constitutes the climactic moment in the story, when all the questions about Jekyll's relationship to Hyde suddenly come to a resolution.

    Stevenson heightens the effect of his climax by describing the scene in intensely vivid language. When he depicts Hyde as "staring with injected eyes" and suggests the dreadful contortions of his features as they "melt and alter," he superbly evokes the ghastliness of the moment of transformation. As this passage emphasizes, the true horror of Jekyll and Hyde's secret is not that they are two sides of the same person, each persona able to assert itself at will, but that each is actually trapped within the grip of the other, fighting for dominance. The transformation process appears fittingly violent and ravaging, causing the metamorphosing body to "reel," "stagger," and "gasp." Indeed, by this point in the novel, Jekyll is losing ground to Hyde, and, correspondingly, emerges "half fainting," as if "restored from death."

QUOTATIONS

4.   It was on the moral side, and in my own person, that I
      learned to recognise the thorough and primitive
      duality of man; I saw that, of the two natures that
      contended in the field of my consciousness, even if I
      could rightly be said to be either, it was only because I
      was radically both; and from an early date . . . I had
      learned to dwell with pleasure, as a beloved
      daydream, on the thought of the separation of
      these elements.

This quotation appears midway through Chapter 10, "Henry
Jekyll's Full Statement of the Case," which consists of the letter that
Jekyll leaves for Utterson. The letter allows us finally to glimpse the
events of the novel from the inside. In this passage, Jekyll discusses
the years leading up to his discovery of the potion that transforms
him into Hyde. He summarizes his theory of humanity's dual
nature, which states that human beings are half virtuous and half
criminal, half moral and half amoral. Jekyll's goal in his experiments is to separate these two elements, creating a being of pure
good and a being of pure evil. In this way he seeks to free his good
side from dark urges while liberating his wicked side from the pangs
of conscience. Ultimately, however, Jekyll succeeds only in separating out Hyde, his evil half, while he himself remains a mix of good
and evil. And eventually, of course, Hyde begins to predominate,
until Jekyll ceases to exist and only Hyde remains. This outcome
suggests a possible fallacy in Jekyll's original assumptions. Perhaps
he did not possess an equally balanced good half and evil half, as he
thought. The events of the novel imply that the dark side (Hyde) is
far stronger than the rest of Jekyll—so strong that, once sent free,
this side takes him over completely.

QUOTATIONS

5. [B]ut I was still cursed with my duality of purpose; and as the first edge of my penitence wore off, the lower side of me, so long indulged, so recently chained down, began to growl for licence. Not that I dreamed of resuscitating Hyde; . . . no, it was in my own person that I was once more tempted to trifle with my conscience. . . .

[However,] this brief condescension to my evil finally destroyed the balance of my soul. And yet I was not alarmed; the fall seemed natural, like a return to the old days before I had made discovery. It was a fine . . . day. . . . I sat in the sun on a bench; the animal within me licking the chops of memory; the spiritual side a little drowsed, promising subsequent penitence, but not yet moved to begin. After all, I reflected, I was like my neighbours; and then I smiled, comparing myself with other men, comparing my active goodwill with the lazy cruelty of their neglect. And at the very moment of that vainglorious thought, a qualm came over me, a horrid nausea and the most deadly shuddering. . . . I began to be aware of a change in the temper of my thoughts, a greater boldness, a contempt of danger, a solution of the bonds of obligation. I looked down; my clothes hung formlessly on my shrunken limbs; the hand that lay on my knee was corded and hairy. I was once more Edward Hyde.

QUOTATIONS

These words appear in Jekyll's confession, near the end of Chapter 10, and they mark the point at which Hyde finally and inalterably begins to dominate the Jekyll-Hyde relationship; Jekyll begins to transform into his darker self spontaneously, without the aid of his potion, and while wide awake. In the particular instance described in the passage, it only takes a single prideful thought to effect the transformation—although that thought comes on the heels of a Jekyll's dip into his old, pre-Hyde debauchery. As elsewhere, the novel gives no details here of the exact sins involved in Jekyll's "brief condescension to evil," and thus when he mentions "the animal within me licking the chops of memory," we are left to imagine what dark deeds Jekyll remembers. Again, the language of this passage emphasizes Jekyll's dualistic theory of human nature, as he contrasts "the animal within me" to his "spiritual side." And the text deliberately presents Hyde's body as animal-like, especially in the reference to a "corded and hairy" hand. In addition, Stevenson describes Jekyll's longing as a "growl for licence," which, ironically, is reminiscent of animals communicating with each other. In a novel intentionally devoid of billowy language and concerned more with providing a record than with developing verbal description, Jekyll can be most vocally expressive of his desires when he longs to transform into Hyde. As Hyde, he loses the conscious abilities to form language completely, falling victim to the instincts within and losing the ability to recall exactly what is happening. The above description implies that Jekyll, in becoming Hyde, is regressing into the primitive and coming closer to the violent, amoral world of animals.

KEY FACTS

FULL TITLE
The Strange Case of Dr. Jekyll and Mr. Hyde

AUTHOR
Robert Louis Stevenson

TYPE OF WORK
Novel

GENRE
Gothic mystery story

LANGUAGE
English

TIME AND PLACE WRITTEN
1885, Bournemouth, England

DATE OF FIRST PUBLICATION
January 1886

PUBLISHER
Longmans, Green and Co.

NARRATOR
The narrator is anonymous and speaks in the third person. Dr. Lanyon and Dr. Jekyll each narrate one chapter of the novel via a confessional letter.

POINT OF VIEW
For most of the novel, the narrative follows Utterson's point of view; in the last two chapters, Lanyon and Jekyll report their experiences from their own perspectives.

TONE
Mysterious; serious

TENSE
Past

SETTING (TIME)
The late nineteenth century

SETTING (PLACE)
London

PROTAGONIST
Henry Jekyll

MAJOR CONFLICT
Jekyll attempts to keep his dark half, Edward Hyde,
under control and then to prevent himself from becoming
Hyde permanently.

RISING ACTION
Utterson attempts to discover the truth about the Jekyll-
Hyde relationship.

CLIMAX
One could argue for two different climaxes. The moment when
Utterson breaks down the door to Jekyll's laboratory and finds
Hyde's corpse constitutes a climax in that Utterson finally
admits and accepts that something terribly wrong has taken
place. But one might also see the novel's climax as arising within
Lanyon's letter, at the moment that he witnesses Hyde's
transformation into Jekyll and the mysterious connection
between the personas is finally explained.

FALLING ACTION
Utterson leaves Jekyll's laboratory, goes home, and reads the
letters from Lanyon and Jekyll, which explain all.

THEMES
The duality of human nature; the importance of reputation

MOTIFS
Violence against innocents; silence; urban terror

SYMBOLS
Jekyll's house and laboratory; Hyde's physical appearance

FORESHADOWING
While a general mood of impending disaster pervades the novel,
there are few instances of explicit foreshadowing.

STUDY QUESTIONS & ESSAY TOPICS

STUDY QUESTIONS

1. *How does Utterson perceive the relationship between Jekyll and Hyde for most of the novel? Is his interpretation understandable? What are the limits of his knowledge?*

Utterson spends much of the novel gathering evidence, in an informal fashion, about the Jekyll-Hyde relationship. All the evidence he collects points to the idea that Hyde is blackmailing Jekyll, which would explain why Jekyll turns pale whenever Hyde is mentioned. It would also explain why Hyde uses a personal check from Jekyll to pay off the parents of the girl he tramples and why Jekyll seems to be protecting Hyde after the Carew murder. Most important, it would explain why Jekyll has made a will that leaves his money to Hyde in the event of his death or "disappearance." Indeed, the will's reference to disappearance leads Utterson to assume that Hyde plans to murder the Jekyll; there seems little else that could cause a respectable doctor simply to vanish. All of Utterson's deductions fit the facts at hand. They construe the Hyde-Jekyll connection as nothing more than the grip of a common criminal on his victim. They serve to make sense of a baffling situation, and they are reasonable.

But, of course, the reasonable nature of Utterson's deductions proves precisely their downfall. Utterson remains so adamantly rational and sensible that he never once admits the possibility of a supernatural explanation. He is the embodiment of the Victorian mind, which is either unable or unwilling to acknowledge the existence of the perverse or transgressive.

2. *Paying particular attention to Stevenson's descriptions of the city at night, discuss how Stevenson uses descriptive passages to evoke a mood of dread.*

At various junctures in *Dr. Jekyll and Mr. Hyde*, Stevenson uses vivid descriptions to evoke a sense of the uncanny and the supernatural, and of looming disaster. He first employs this technique in the opening scene, when Enfield relates his story of witnessing Hyde trample a little girl—a night when the streets were so empty that he began "to long for the sight of a policeman."

This notion of the city as a fearful landscape recurs throughout the novel. After hearing the tale of Mr. Hyde, Utterson suffers from dreams in which Hyde stalks through "labyrinths of lamp-lighted city," crushing children and whispering evil into Jekyll's ears. In Utterson's vision, London becomes a nightmare city, a place of terror where Hyde can perpetrate his crimes unchecked. The nightmare city reappears in Utterson's later, waking description of London. Leading the police to Hyde's apartment through a foggy pre-dawn, Utterson watches the mist swirl and transform the neighborhood into "a district of some city in a nightmare," bringing a "touch" of "terror" even to the stolid policemen.

By the novel's final scene, these cityscapes connote not only terror but also foreboding of even more horrifying dangers. When Poole fetches Utterson to Jekyll's house, the wildness of the night and the empty streets fill the lawyer with "a crushing anticipation of calamity." In all these descriptions, Stevenson creates a perceptual dread that reinforces the conceptual horror of his subject matter.

3. *Discuss the narrative approach in the novel. What characterizes the way that events are reported? How does this method of narrative contribute to the thematic development of the novel?*

Much of *Dr. Jekyll and Mr. Hyde* is written in a brisk, businesslike, and factual way. Dry and forthright, the text often resembles a police report more than a novel. This colorlessness derives in part from the personality of Mr. Utterson, through whose eyes most of the story is told. Proper and upright, Utterson approaches the events with a desire to preserve any possible trace of orderliness or rationality in them. But the narrative's dry manner also seems to arise from the text itself. The original title of the novel, *The Strange Case of Dr. Jekyll and Mr. Hyde,* as well as chapter headings—including "Incident of the Letter" and "Incident at the Window"—seem to reveal an attitude of scientific detachment within the very structure of the novel. When the text presents the letters of Lanyon and Jekyll almost as if they were pieces of evidence, the story itself seems to become something of a scientific proof.

The attitude of formality and propriety in the narrative contrasts sharply with its mystical and uncanny content. With its prim demeanor, the text could be seen as attempting to repress or deny the subject matter that lurks inside it. Stevenson implies that a similar dynamic is at work in the Victorian Britain that he inhabits and portrays. The phenomenon plays itself out on the individual scale as well, of course—the existence of Hyde in the novel testifies to the existence of an evil or primitive aspect within each one of us, just barely hidden beneath a polite, unruffled exterior.

Suggested Essay Topics

1. Analyze the different stages of Jekyll's experimentation with the Hyde persona. How do his feelings regarding the transformations change?

2. How does Jekyll interpret his relationship to Hyde? Do you agree with his understanding? Why or why not?

3. Examine the role of the minor characters in the novel, including Lanyon, Enfield, Carew, and Poole. How does Utterson's connection to each of these men serve to advance the plot?

4. At one point in the novel, Hyde is described as a "troglodyte." To what does this term refer? What was its significance in Victorian England? How does it relate to the themes of the novel?

5. Why do you think Stevenson chose to tell the story from Utterson's point of view rather than use Jekyll's from the beginning? How does this choice increase the suspense of the novel?

REVIEW & RESOURCES

QUIZ

1. What is Utterson's profession?

   A. Lawyer
   B. Doctor
   C. Priest
   D. Detective

2. With whom does Utterson take a weekly walk?

   A. Jekyll
   B. Lanyon
   C. Enfield
   D. Poole

3. What did Enfield see Hyde do late one night?

   A. Break into Jekyll's house
   B. Trample a girl
   C. Shoot a man
   D. Steal bread

4. Whom does Jekyll's will initially specify as his heir?

   A. Poole
   B. Lanyon
   C. Enfield
   D. Hyde

5. Why has Lanyon and Jekyll's friendship cooled?

   A. They had a dispute over Jekyll's scientific inquiries
   B. They both fell in love with the same woman
   C. Lanyon found Jekyll's run-down laboratory unsettling
   D. Jekyll stole Lanyon's research

6. How does Utterson first meet Hyde?

    A. He goes to Hyde's home
    B. They meet at a dinner party
    C. Utterson stakes out the door to Jekyll's laboratory, where Hyde has been known to come
    D. Hyde comes to Utterson with a legal question

7. How do the characters in the novel describe Hyde?

    A. They cannot describe him; they are struck by lightning when they utter his name
    B. They say he is ugly and deformed but cannot say exactly why
    C. They say he looks oddly similar to Jekyll—like a warped version of him
    D. They say he has an ugly scar across his face

8. When Utterson tells Jekyll that he has "been learning something of young Hyde," how does Jekyll respond?

    A. He laughs and says that Utterson is lying
    B. He claims never to have met Hyde
    C. He admits everything
    D. He turns pale and begs Utterson to change the subject

9. What does a servant girl witness from a window?

    A. Hyde murdering Sir Danvers Carew
    B. Jekyll and Hyde meeting in secret
    C. Jekyll transforming into Hyde
    D. Hyde trampling a little child

10. Who leads the police to Hyde's home?

    A. Jekyll
    B. A servant girl
    C. Utterson
    D. Enfield

11. What is Poole's position?

    A.   He is Jekyll's lab assistant

    B.   He is Jekyll's butler

    C.   He is Utterson's clerk

    D.   He is a detective

12. What happens to Hyde after the Carew murder?

    A.   His body is found in the river

    B.   He flees the country

    C.   He kills Jekyll

    D.   He disappears

13. What happens to Jekyll after the Carew murder?

    A.   He becomes more sociable and devotes himself to good works

    B.   He enters into a friendship with Enfield

    C.   He abandons science

    D.   He flees the country

14. What does Mr. Guest tell Utterson about the handwriting on the letter from Hyde?

    A.   It has been forged

    B.   It is a woman's handwriting

    C.   It belongs to Jekyll

    D.   It belongs to a left-handed person

15. What does Lanyon give Utterson before he dies?

    A.   A box, not to be opened until Lanyon's death

    B.   A letter, not to be opened until Jekyll's death or disappearance

    C.   A small fortune

    D.   A mysterious vial

16. In the weeks following his dinner party, what happens to Jekyll?

   A. He slowly poisons himself
   B. He begins plotting to kill Utterson
   C. He flees the country
   D. He locks himself in his laboratory and refuses to see anyone

17. Where do Enfield and Utterson see Jekyll one day during his seclusion?

   A. At Lanyon's funeral
   B. At the window of his laboratory
   C. In Hyde's apartment
   D. On a foggy street

18. Who summons Utterson to Jekyll's house near the end of the novel?

   A. Enfield
   B. Jekyll himself
   C. Poole
   D. Hyde

19. Why do the servants think that the man in the laboratory is not Jekyll?

   A. His voice is different from Jekyll's
   B. Jekyll is out of the country
   C. Jekyll is dead
   D. Jekyll never goes in the laboratory

20. Who does Utterson find in the laboratory after breaking down the door?

   A. Enfield
   B. No one
   C. Jekyll, lying dead
   D. Hyde, lying dead

21. What horrifying event does Lanyon write about having witnessed?

    A.   The death of Danvers Carew
    B.   Jekyll transforming into Hyde
    C.   Hyde transforming into Jekyll
    D.   Utterson killing himself

22. Who is Hyde?

    A.   Jekyll's insane brother, whom he has tried to keep locked in the attic
    B.   Jekyll's son born out of wedlock
    C.   Jekyll's dark side, embodied in a separate being
    D.   Jekyll in disguise

23. What brings Hyde into being?

    A.   A potion, concocted by Jekyll
    B.   A magic book
    C.   A genie
    D.   Incantations

24. Initially, why does Jekyll turn himself into Hyde?

    A.   Poole forces him to do so
    B.   He wants to escape his nagging wife
    C.   He wants to kill Carew and Utterson
    D.   He enjoys doing so

25. How does Jekyll deal with Hyde in the end?

    A.   He has a priest exorcize Hyde
    B.   He shoots Hyde
    C.   He realizes the folly of becoming Hyde and decides to live the rest of his life as Jekyll
    D.   Involuntarily, he becomes Hyde permanently, and then Hyde kills himself

Answer Key:
1: A; 2: C; 3: B; 4: D; 5: A; 6: C; 7: B; 8: D; 9: A; 10: C; 11: B; 12: D; 13: A; 14: C; 15: B; 16: D; 17: B; 18: C; 19: A; 20: D; 21: C; 22: C; 23: A; 24: D; 25: D

Suggestions for Further Reading

HAMMOND, J. R. *A Robert Louis Stevenson Companion: A Guide to the Novels, Essays, and Short Stories.* London: Macmillan, 1984.

HUBBARD, TOM. *Seeking Mr. Hyde: Studies in Robert Louis Stevenson, Symbolism, Myth, and the Pre-Modern.* Frankfurt: Peter Lang, 1995.

MAIXNER, PAUL, ed. *Robert Louis Stevenson, the Critical Heritage.* Boston: Routledge & Kegan Paul, 1981.

NABOKOV, VLADIMIR. *Lectures on Literature.* New York: Harcourt Brace Jovanovich, 1980.

NOBLE, ANDREW, ed. *Robert Louis Stevenson.* Totowa, New Jersey: Barnes and Noble, 1983.

SAPOSNIK, IRVING S. *Robert Louis Stevenson.* New York: Twayne Publishers, 1974.

VEEDER, WILLIAM R., and GORDON HIRSCH. DR. JEKYLL AND MR. HYDE *After One Hundred Years.* Chicago: University of Chicago Press, 1988.

A Note on the Type

The typeface used in SparkNotes study guides is Sabon, created by master typographer Jan Tschichold in 1964. Tschichold revolutionized the field of graphic design twice: first with his use of asymmetrical layouts and sanserif type in the 1930s when he was affiliated with the Bauhaus, then by abandoning assymetry and calling for a return to the classic ideals of design. Sabon, his only extant typeface, is emblematic of his latter program: Tschichold's design is a recreation of the types made by Claude Garamond, the great French typographer of the Renaissance, and his contemporary Robert Granjon. Fittingly, it is named for Garamond's apprentice, Jacques Sabon.

SPARKNOTES
TEST PREPARATION
GUIDES

The SparkNotes team figured it was time to cut standardized tests down to size. We've studied the tests for you, so that SparkNotes test prep guides are:

Smarter:
Packed with critical-thinking skills and test-
taking strategies that will improve your score.

Better:
Fully up to date, covering all new features of the tests,
with study tips on every type of question.

Faster:
Our books cover exactly what you need to
know for the test. No more, no less.

SparkNotes Guide to the SAT & PSAT
SparkNotes Guide to the SAT & PSAT—Deluxe Internet Edition
SparkNotes Guide to the ACT
SparkNotes Guide to the ACT—Deluxe Internet Edition
SparkNotes Guide to the SAT II Writing
SparkNotes Guide to the SAT II U.S. History
SparkNotes Guide to the SAT II Math Ic
SparkNotes Guide to the SAT II Math IIc
SparkNotes Guide to the SAT II Biology
SparkNotes Guide to the SAT II Physics

SparkNotes Study Guides: